Recipe For Leadership

Ed Gagnon

Bloomington, IN  Milton Keynes, UK

AuthorHouse™
1663 Liberty Drive, Suite 200
Bloomington, IN 47403
www.authorhouse.com
Phone: 1-800-839-8640

AuthorHouse™ UK Ltd.
500 Avebury Boulevard
Central Milton Keynes, MK9 2BE
www.authorhouse.co.uk
Phone: 08001974150

First published by AuthorHouse 6/20/2006

ISBN: 1-4259-3662-8 (sc)

Printed in the United States of America
Bloomington, Indiana

This book is printed on acid-free paper.

The Recipe

Driving Accomplishments
When people achieve meaningful
accomplishments their self-esteem increases.

Providing knowledge, truth, involvement, support and accountability.
When people are treated like partners they perform
like partners – they have a sense of ownership.

Values & Attributes
When people respect the values
and attributes of a manager they will follow
this individual's lead with eagerness.

- Integrity
- Courage
- Unselfishness
- Accepting of responsibility
- Energetic
- Sincere
- Challenging
- Inspirational
- Trustworthy
- Trusting in others
- Decisiveness

A Leader is Born

<u>Adding the Ingredients to the Recipe</u>

When a manager drives people to seek out accomplishments this manager is inspiring people to achieve great things. When a manager treats people like intelligent contributors to the organization this manager is encouraging people to fulfill the role of intelligent contributors. When each individual's need for high self-esteem and self-actualization is cherished and supported this manager will be trusted and followed with confidence. When people are challenged and supported to become the best that they can be, they know their manager is a true leader who has their best interests in mind.

These are some of the ingredients in the Recipe for Leadership that can help to change a manager into a leader.

In this recipe, values such as integrity and trustworthiness are the pot of water in which the ingredients are mixed. The drive for accomplishments, providing knowledge, truth, involvement, support and accountability are the stock of the recipe. The attributes of the leader such as the courage to be true to one's beliefs, to trust in others, to be sincere in all dealings with people, to be unselfish, self-disciplined, and to have the ability to inspire greatness from others, are some of the spices.

With the application of this recipe managers can become true leaders who create a workforce of partners. These partners work hard to achieve daily accomplishments for their own reasons. These partners enjoy feelings of high self-esteem as a result of their accomplishments. These feelings of high self-esteem provide the fuel for further accomplishments. This self-perpetuating cycle of events provides feelings of fulfillment for the individual and success for the organization.

Effective leaders create a workforce of individuals who each have self-motivating feelings about the accomplishments each is achieving for a collective cause greater than the single individual. Effective leaders know it is all about feelings. Effective leaders know that feelings are more important than facts.

Feelings drive actions – facts record them.

Effective leaders therefore drive and support accomplishments.

Leaders know that if an organization is to reach its potential each individual within the organization must reach his and her potential. In order for each individual to reach his or her potential it is essential that each individual believe he or she can make a difference.

Each individual is capable of believing this but only if the leader believes and lives this. The best way to show this belief in people is to challenge them to greatness.

By challenging people to be the best that they can be, the leader is clearly stating that he or she believes in this person and that the individual makes a difference.

Once challenged it is essential that the individual is supported.

Effective support is achieved by educating each individual, helping to remove obstacles as appropriate, and holding each person accountable for their actions.

The leader and the people must understand that no one makes it alone and therefore seeks out associations that support each individual's goals. The leader that knows and practices this belief helps to provide this beneficial association by applying all of his or her given authority and all of his or her passion for excellence to the success of each individual.

As people become involved and successful their feelings of empowerment will grow and more accomplishments will result.

Through challenge and support people will seek out greatness and the leader will be born.

When we talk about support, however, it is important to remember the difference between doing things for people and doing things with people.

The accomplishments must belong to the individual, not the leader.

Therefore support looks something like this:

- trust in the ability of the individual,
- trustworthiness on the part of the leader,
- consideration for the uniqueness of each individual,

- guidance in the planning stages from the leader,
- inspiration in the face of difficulties,
- help to maintain focus on the process and end in mind,
- emphasis on self-discipline from the leader,
- encouragement to remain open to new ideas from the leader,
- insistence of complete honesty from all involved,
- recognition of the need for courage,
- unselfishness on the part of all involved,
- accepting of responsibility from all involved,
- decisiveness from all involved,
- enjoying the successes and recognizing individual contributions.

Examine the following statement:

"Solving problems, big problems and little problems, will not halt the decline of American industry, nor will expansion and use of computers, gadgets, and robotic machinery. Benefits from massive new machines also constitute a vain new hope. Massive immediate expansion in teaching of statistical methods to production workers is not the answer either, nor wholesale flashes of quality circles. All these activities make their contribution, but they only prolong the life of the patient; they cannot halt the decline.

Only the transformation of the American style of management can halt the decline and give American industry a chance to lead the world again."
W. Edwards Deming
"Out of Crisis"

Clearly the late Dr. Deming is suggesting that we do not need more management programs – but rather a transformation of management's styles and beliefs.

Clearly he is stating that the programs we undertake are less important than management's values, leadership and ability to inspire greatness in others.

What do you believe?

Douglas McGregor's theory of X and Y states that people have basic assumptions about others and these beliefs influence how people act toward one another. Managers categorized as theory X believe that all people are innately lazy and unreliable – that people will try to do as little as possible. Theory X people believe that controls placed on people by management are the only way management can get people to do the proper things.

Contrary to the X theory is the Y theory. This theory professes that people are basically self-motivated, able to self-direct, and can be creative without management controls. What do you believe?

Frederick Taylor believed that management must assume the responsibility for detailing the methods and procedures for performing work. These well-defined procedures are to be closely followed by employees. He also believed most people were incapable of managing and motivating themselves. Clearly he leaned toward theory X.

Max Weber placed his emphasis on the specialization of people. That is, that each person is only good at one or two things and it is management's job to ensure they pick the right person for the right job. He also believed in many detailed written procedures, policies, and procedures to control people's behavior.

John Locke believed people will do what is right simply because it is right. He believed everyone has it within him or herself to self-motivate and self-manage.

Freud believed people have basic biological and genetic factors that form their personality and consequential behavior and that management has very little influence over these factors.

It is my belief that many of the past and present beliefs about the management of people are partially correct with some of the people some of the time. We could all cite examples of interactions in which one or more of the beliefs stated above were correct, and when some were incorrect.

But I don't think that exercise will get us anywhere, nor will it provide any more guidance than that of knowing managers must be flexible, adaptable and have a wide variety of experiences to draw upon. Additionally, knowing how to manage each individual at a given point of time, in a given situation, would probably require a degree in psychology.

I have a more basic belief. I believe that more emphasis needs to be placed on the higher level needs of people, and that it is management's responsibility to help fulfill these needs by becoming real leaders.

Dr. Abraham Maslow's belief that people must satisfy their basic needs for safety, security and social acceptance before being able to seek satisfaction for their higher needs of self-esteem and self-actualization makes a good deal of sense to me. But I think it goes further than this.

Without the influence of inspiring leadership even the best people will not live up to potential. People can satisfy their basic needs of safety, security and social acceptance with a minimum of outside help. But without inspiring leadership they cannot continue the journey to the higher level needs of self-esteem and self-actualization.

Real leaders provide people with the sustenance they need to achieve feelings of fulfillment. Real leaders have true concern for each individual. Real leaders show this by encouraging people to accept challenges. Only in this way can an individual achieve a meaningful accomplishment. Only in this way can an individual feel good about him or herself. Real leaders drive people to be the best they can be.

I once knew a department manager who was extremely skilled at all the technical aspects of his job. He had a vast knowledge of the trade and a keen intellect. He was a respected individual. Everyone believed he and his department would be very successful with him at the helm.

Yet as time went on his department continually fell short of its goals. In spite of all he knew, he was unable to lead his department to excellence. No one seemed to know why this was so, but when one talked with the people in the department it became clear that they were not experiencing the good feelings that are a result of accomplishments.

They were suffering the effects of low self-esteem and a lack of fulfillment.

It became clear that this department manager was not comfortable sharing his knowledge and inspiring others to greatness. He did not involve, empower or encourage people to accept challenges. The people lacked knowledge, truth and direction.

Because the people were performing poorly and because it was his nature, this department manager began to distrust even more than before. The lack of trust led to more over-controlling of all activities, but no matter how many controls he implemented, the people continued to perform poorly. He did not realize that it is inspiration, not control, that ensures great performance.

This department manager was eventually removed from the position. The new manager was quite different. He did not have the great technical knowledge of the former manager but he was clearly a more people-oriented individual who gained their respect and support very quickly.

This manager spent a large portion of his time sharing his knowledge and passing on information necessary to select a direction. He challenged people to change and grow, and supported them on the journey.

He involved people in goal setting and the methods to accomplish the goals. He held people accountable by recognizing both the good and not so good things people were accomplishing.

The results were astounding. The people's self-esteem began to grow with each accomplishment that was made. He and his entire department began to realize a sense of fulfillment. The organization benefited tremendously and the motivation to continue the improvements was self-sustaining.

The new manager achieved <u>"Leadership"</u>.

He inspired people to achieve greatness. He effectively applied the ingredients and spices of the recipe for leadership. He and his people enjoyed the rewards.

It starts with a belief:
- Everyone has a need to achieve accomplishments.
- Everyone needs the help of inspiring leadership.

The belief becomes reality through:
- Challenges
- Support
- Encouragement
- Accomplishments
- Acknowledgement

It is made possible by:
- Knowledge
- Truth
- Trust

- Inspiration
- Focus
- Decisiveness
- Energy

It results in feelings of:
- High Self-Esteem
- Fulfillment

Applying the Recipe for Leadership

The need for someone to accept responsibility for organizational results and initiate actions to improve these results has been the primary reason for management's existence throughout time.

Some of the responsibilities may be:

Ensuring:
- processes are effective
- systems are effective
- policies are adequate
- equipment is adequate
- budgets are adhered to
- schedules are adhered to
- R&D is properly focused
- engineering is effective
- quality is high
- efficiencies are achieved
- customer deliveries are on-time
- safe work practices are in place

Running through this entire list is one common thread. That one thread is people. All these functions and activities require the effectiveness of people for their success.

Management working through people for people will effectively accomplish all other responsibilities. No matter how automated a company may be, people make things happen. People develop, implement and maintain all things – even automation.

If you want to become an effective manager, use the ingredients of effective leadership.

- share your thoughts with people,
- spend time and energy helping others to grow and become more successful,
- help people at all levels of the organization to understand that the achievement of individual needs will result in organizational success – and organizational success contributes to the satisfaction of the needs of each individual,
- work to create a positive, can-do culture,
- manage in a manner that supports the belief that an organization can be no greater than its people – and people can be no greater than their self-esteem,
- be sensitive to the needs of people – show true concern,
- provide people with knowledge, truth, involvement, empowerment, support, decisiveness and account-ability,
- take every opportunity to foster an environment in which feelings of fulfillment flourish.

The transition from manager to leader requires insight, a change in activities, trust in people, trust in one's own beliefs, and the courage to follow through. You will need to spend time creating a culture rather than trying to control every activity.

The Culture:

- <u>People sharing knowledge and feelings without apprehension.</u> It starts with you. You need to have the courage to become vulnerable. People need to see the caring, human side of you. You are not permissive toward improper behavior – you do not allow actions that are not in the best interests of the organization – but you do care about each individual and sincerely appreciate the uniqueness and contributions of each person. When you really care about people you insist they live up to their potential and do not do anything that will ultimately harm themselves, the organization, or its people.

- <u>People respecting and understanding the importance of each individual's self-esteem.</u> Your respect for people should be clearly evident. Once it is made visible for everyone to see, it will be emulated. People will learn that each individual has a great deal to offer when they are experiencing feelings of high self-esteem. They learn this from you.

- <u>People eager to be involved in the planning and execution of ideas.</u> You encourage involvement and do not punish those who fall short of expectations unless for reasons of complacency or intent. People are allowed to give their opinions even if they are not popular. People are recognized for their efforts and contributions.

- <u>People treated like, and feeling like, partners in pursuit of excellence.</u> You share problems and ideas with people as you would with a partner. Through the knowledge and truth people receive, they gain feelings of ownership and responsibility. They want to help. Everyone is respected as a contributor, a partner, and people rise to the occasion.

- <u>People having the desire to take personal risks for the good of the organization and its people.</u> You support people and treat everyone fairly so they know they are not threatened. They are not afraid to participate. They willingly take risks.

- <u>People making personal sacrifices for the good of the organization and its people.</u> You are eager to give of yourself and people see your willingness to accept the burden. They know they will be recognized for the good things they do and they have learned that sacrificing for a cause greater than themselves brings feelings of high self-esteem and fulfillment.

You can develop this culture by developing yourself. Try being more:

- <u>Generous</u> with your time. Stop what you are doing when someone wants to talk with you. Listen actively to people. Listening attentively is one of the greatest compliments one person can give to another. Never treat people as interruptions of your job – people are your job.

- <u>Inspiring and optimistic</u> about everything. Look for the opportunity in every problem. Become the model of can-do. Never view problems as pervasive obstacles. Never accept the role of a victim who has no control over the events of his or her life.

- <u>Decisive</u>. Become the example of how to stamp out complacency and ambivalence. Be aggressive for what is right. Take actions as appropriate to circumstances.

- Empathetic when people are unsure or unaware. Help people to help them selves by teaching them that failure frequently precedes success. Show them trust and give them room to act.

- Trustworthy always. Never betray anyone's trust in you. Always be completely truthful – even when you don't think you have to be. Honesty is the foundation of trust – trust is the foundation of leadership and a healthy organization. It is better to say you cannot discuss an issue than it is to lie about it.

- Trusting in others until proven wrong. Start out by always believing in people and their abilities. People's ability to believe in themselves is often based upon their leader's belief in them. The belief people have in them selves can be the difference between their success or failure.

- Confident in yourself. The people with whom you work need you to be confident of the direction you have chosen for them and the organization. People need to be confident that the culture you are seeking is best for everyone. No matter how many minor setbacks you have, go forward with the confidence that yours is the better way.

- Open in all your dealings. Do not hold back anything. Except for information that could be harmful to the company if known to people outside the company, you should share what you know with eagerness. Show people who you are and in what you believe. Share your values with people and let them see that you are true to them. Share your weaknesses and concerns so that people can feel closer to you. It is the sharing of weaknesses – not strengths – that brings people closer together.

- <u>Competent</u> in both technical and managerial skills. Work hard to become more expert in your field. Management excellence requires you to fulfill all your responsibilities.

- <u>Friendly</u> and pleasant. Say hello with a smile every morning and wish everyone a good night at the end of each day. Show you care by going out of your way to be available at these two crucial times. Be gracious. Be a nice person.

- <u>Proud</u> of your accomplishments and the people with whom you work. Be proud that you are helping to satisfy the needs of the organization and its people. Be proud that you are a good person, doing good things, getting good results. Be proud of the accomplishments the people are making in this progressive environment.

- <u>Concerned</u> for others always. Make the needs of others a priority. Satisfaction of each individual's need for achieving accomplishments will ensure your success and that of the organization. It is simply right to be this way.

- <u>Courageous</u> in your beliefs and actions. Courage is the mark of a leader. Courage to follow your own path. Courage to lead through inspiration rather than controls. Courage to be vulnerable. Courage to trust others. Courage to be the person you have chosen to be.

- <u>Filled with integrity always.</u> A manager can only become a leader if he or she is filled with integrity. You must be honest even when you don't have to be. Your words must be beyond reproach. Your integrity makes you the pillar of correctness.
- <u>Energetic</u> in everything you do. Always focused. Hardworking and without complaint. An example of a superior work ethic.
- <u>Passionate</u> about the things you are accomplishing. Your passion for a better way to manage – to become a leader – inspires others to follow and provides you with results that sustain your passion.

The culture you create will determine your success at becoming an effective leader.

<u>Nothing is more important.</u>

Inspiration & Sincerity
(Ingredients in the recipe for leadership)

A manager cannot and should not expect a person to eagerly support his or her plans simply because the person is being paid. When a person's only motivation for working is to earn money, he or she will usually do the minimum amount necessary to stay out of harms way and still get the money. There is little reason to do more. Without an opportunity to fulfill the higher level need of self-esteem through involvement and achievement, work can be burdensome and uninspiring. Without the opportunity to gain knowledge, truth, feelings of empowerment, support and accountability, a person can wander aimlessly.

If an organization is to experience its potential, each individual within the organization must realize his or her potential. Leaders must rise above the shallow management style that relies on paychecks or rewards or punishments (the lower level needs identified by Abraham Maslow). Leaders must help to develop a culture in which each individual is able to achieve the higher level needs of self-esteem and self-actualization.

Effective leaders know that to develop a motivated and capable team they must do much more than devise plans, direct activities and punish people who make mistakes.

Effective leaders seek to develop a workforce that

cares about the work it does – cares about the organization – cares about the people within the organization – and is willing to sacrifice some comfort for the good of the organization and its people.

Effective leaders develop this ideal workforce by first developing themselves. They share knowledge and truth. They involve, empower and support people. They help people to contribute meaningful accomplishments. They care for people and show their true concern for people by helping each individual reach his or her potential.

Effective leaders know that people:
- must believe they can make a difference,
- must be provided with knowledge and truth,
- must be given a chance to become involved,
- must be supported in order to achieve meaningful accomplishments.

Effective leaders foster feelings of importance in each individual by asking each person for his or her opinion, asking each individual to become involved, and listening in an empathetic manner.

Leaders have a passion to influence, balanced by a positive belief in people. They care about people.

They stir in the spices of leadership.
- They challenge people,
- They help to educate people,
- They encourage people,
- They support people,
- They hold people accountable,

- They bring people to a level they would not have been able to achieve without their leadership,
- They are true to their values of integrity, courage and unselfishness.

I once knew a manager who was hired to turn around the very poor performance of a 300-person department. He appeared very astute and forceful. He had a great deal of self-confidence that spilled over into everything he did and to everyone with whom he came in contact.

Yet, he failed. Within 6-months it became clear that his department was no better than it had been, and in fact, may have been worse.

This department manager was not a very inspiring person. People working within the department felt like he tolerated rather than appreciated them. He rarely asked people for their advice and he was consistently non-supportive of anyone who was having difficulty. The people and the management team felt alone, confused, and unaware of how to resolve the many problems within the department. This department manager had to be replaced.

The new manager immediately began to conduct small group meetings with the people and management team. He shared with them the situation and some of the greatest needs of the department. He asked for their opinions. He challenged them to make a difference. He supported their efforts and recognized their accomplishments.

At first they did not know what to make of this open, caring and supportive management style. Because it was something they had not yet experienced they were afraid to say and do the wrong thing. The new manager was very accepting and gracious about everything they said and tried to do. Within a couple of months people began opening up and things started to happen.

As the department's performance improved credit was openly given to the management team and the people doing the work. With their self-esteem high, their motivation to do more increased. A self-perpetuating cycle of improvements and good feelings took hold and the department became one of the best in the company.

What was the difference? What did the new department manager do that the old one did not?

- He asked people to help.
- He listened and supported.
- He mixed in the ingredients for leadership.
- He built trust.
- He created a positive culture.
- He inspired people to make great accomplishments.

Trust

(An ingredient in the recipe for leadership)

When we speak of a person being trusted in the workplace we are really speaking of a person who is perceived to have integrity.

If you want trust you must give truth.

The first and most important value that people look for in a leader is truthfulness. If a manager fails this test, the manager will not become a leader.

It is important that you apply all the ingredients for leadership – but as you do, you will only be as successful as you are truthful. Your integrity is interwoven into everything you do. It is your integrity – your unquestionable honesty – that will ensure all other ingredients will interact properly.

If you want to become a true leader, you must have true integrity.

Trust that is based on integrity is different than trust that is based on feelings. The trust a leader is seeking is the trust of correctness in all activities. People will understand that trust based on integrity means that there may be times when you will take remedial actions toward a person who is out of line or not performing well. Not taking action would be a dishonest thing to do. Not taking action would cause people to lose trust in you.

People expect that a leader will make the hard decisions and carry out the necessary actions for the wellbeing of the entire organization. People will accept that the security of each individual on the job is not based on a leader's blind acceptance, but rather on how each individual performs and accepts his or her responsibilities. People know that true leaders have high standards and cannot be permissive toward those who do not contribute in a positive way. To do so would be to betray the organization, its people and the leader's values. To do so would be dishonest and untrustworthy.

"The only security a person has is his ability to do a job uncommonly well."
Abraham Lincoln

People must believe:
- that management will never be self-serving – rather, it will always do what is right for the organization and its people,
- that management will not allow any single person's interests to be given greater importance than that of the interests of the organization and its people,
- that security is the result of a prosperous organization and an individual's ability to contribute to that prosperity,
- that management will share all it knows so that everyone has the opportunity to grow within the organization.

The task ahead of every manager is to become a true leader of people. When a manager becomes a person filled with integrity he or she can transition to leader. When a manager truly cares about each individual and his or her need for accomplishment and high self-esteem, this person can transition to leader.

<u>Sharing Truth and Knowledge</u>
(An ingredient in the recipe for leadership)

If you want the best, most effective team possible, you need to practice the best, most effective communications possible.

You need to share what you know and believe. You need to share with people as if it were their right to know everything that is going on – because it is.

When you share with people as though you believe it is their right and your obligation, you are treating them as partners rather than employees. When people are treated as partners they act like partners.

Another story: This one is about a supervisor who was the most talented manufacturer of metal components I have ever met. There wasn't anything that he could not design in his head and then skillfully manufacture with his hands. He was truly an artist.

He was also one of the most ineffective supervisors I have ever met. He was promoted because he was very talented, but that is where it ended. He rarely talked to his team, and when he did it was to direct someone to bring him a tool so that he could do his job.

Clearly, it is important that a supervisor know the technical aspects of his or her job, but it is less important than the team knowing the technical aspects of the job. This supervisor never understood this. He thought it was each individual's responsibility to learn as best he or she could, and that each individual was on his or her own to see what could be accomplished.

He would evaluate the talents of each team member, but he never thought of helping them to develop their talents to the level he had achieved. He did his job and they did their jobs, but neither worked together to share knowledge or support each other.

As talented as he was he had the worst performing team in the company. He did not understand that by sharing knowledge and truth, rather than being a single contributor, he and his people could have achieved greatness.

He did appear to care about his people in a paternalistic way. In fact he frequently covered up for individuals by doing jobs for them that they were unable to accomplish. Eventually he tried to do everybody's job because no one was capable of performing the work without help. Naturally, this just made the problem worse.

People were robbed of their opportunity to achieve accomplishments and increase their self-esteem. He continually placed his emphasis on building components rather than creating a culture in which others could learn to become as talented as he was. It was what he was comfortable doing. Like many individuals who gravitate toward doing those things they like to do over those things they should learn to do, he was in a downward spiral.

A supervisor such as this who puts tasks ahead of people will eventually fail. And fail he did. He was deeply hurt by the experience because down deep inside he really did care about the people. He just never knew what they needed and what it took to become an effective leader.

Actually, his manager should have been held responsible as well, because he failed to develop him into the supervisor he needed to become. Because this manager failed to act as a leader, this supervisor failed to become a leader.

<u>The general rule of responsibility goes like this</u>:

When a manager at any level of an organization looks at his or her team and is disappointed with the view, he or she needs to look into a mirror to find both the cause and the solution.

It is always management's responsibility to achieve an effective team. It is always management's responsibility to communicate, empower, support and hold people accountable. It is never the fault of the team if all or most of them are not performing to expectations.

- Do you believe that sharing all your knowledge is your responsibility to the people you manage – not the training department's job?
- Do you believe that sharing general information about the organization is your job – not solely your boss's job?

- Do you believe that sharing your personal values and beliefs is your responsibility?
- Do you share what you believe would be great performance for each individual?
- Do you share the results of each individual's efforts with them?
- Do you guide people to improve?
- Do you share some of your own weaknesses and ask for help?
- Do you informally talk with people in a simple exchange of ideas?
- Do you share your desire to help people be the best they can be?
- Are you open with people?
- Do you practice the 3A's always – (Available-Approachable-Attentive)?
- Do you believe total sharing of all you know is your obligation and people's right?
- Do you continually improve your communication skills?

If you are not willingly sharing knowledge and truth, you are not fulfilling your responsibilities as a manager and will not become a leader. Total sharing requires:

- energy,
- a passion for achieving excellence,
- a true concern for people,
- a true concern for the organization,
- confidence,
- vision,
- determination,

- a positive belief in people,
- a mastery of effective verbal and listening skills.

Effective verbal communications:
- You must have the will to explain yourself whenever you:
  a. start something,
  b. stop something,
  c. change something,
  d. correct something.
- You need to choose your words carefully. The words you choose produce images and feelings in the people listening. They can be powerful tools.
- You need to give people what they need in order to gain their attention. Relate conversations to the individual you are communicating with rather than to yourself. Guide your conversations by applying the big YOU and little me philosophy.
- Always give effort to all conversations. It will be at these moments that people will be evaluating your sincerity, motives and integrity.
- Practice making all conversations concise and to the point. Conversations should be easy to understand. A good vocabulary should be used to help you understand others, not to impress others.
- You should be aware and considerate of the distractions the other person may be having. Distractions could be physical, emotional or intellectual – whatever they are, you must be empathetic to them by either helping the person overcome the distraction, or choosing another time and/or place to have the conversation.

- When conveying a message intended to correct behavior you need to remember that:
a. fear leads to disliking,
b. disliking leads to unwillingness,
c. unwillingness leads to failure,
d. criticism or ridicule most often does not correct – it destroys.

Effective and active listening:
a. It helps you to understand people and be understood in return.
b. It requires you to look past the appearance and presentation of an individual and into the content of his or her message.
c. It requires you to help the person feel comfortable talking with you.
d. It requires patience.
e. It requires self-confidence.
f. It requires you to be open-minded.
g. It requires the energy necessary to focus intently on the message.
h. It requires true concern for people.
i. It requires a positive belief in the value of people.

Unskilled listeners tune out and prejudge the other person – while skilled listeners defer judgement and concentrate on the message.

Unskilled listeners become distracted by grammar, people's appearance and style - while skilled listeners pay attention to the content of the message and are not effected by prejudice.

Unskilled listeners prepare to talk while pretending to listen – while skilled listeners wait for the message to be completed before responding.

Unskilled listeners selectively choose what they want to hear – while skilled listeners pay attention to all points of view.

Unskilled listeners try to listen to multiple messages at the same time – while skilled listeners concentrate on one message at a time.

Unskilled listeners only pretend to be concerned and sincere – while skilled listeners are truly concerned and sincere.

Unskilled listeners give little encouragement to speak – while skilled listeners assure others their thoughts are important.

Unskilled listeners are impatient and seem to have no time to listen – while skilled listeners are patient and always have time to listen.

Unskilled listeners believe listening is less important than influencing others through one-way conversation – while skilled listeners know listening is the highest compliment one can pay to another and therefore is the most effective way to influence others.

Unskilled listeners believe listening is a passive activity – while skilled listeners know active listening requires energy, concentration and persistence.

Unskilled listeners pay little attention to a list such as this – while skilled listeners use this list as a guide to measure and improve their communication and listening skills.

Golden Rules of Communication

Sin: Not listening attentively.
It is insulting.

Rule: Listen with all your energy.
Look directly at the person – show interest through questions, paraphrasing and body language – if you are unable to ask a question or paraphrase a message from someone, you are not actively listening.

Sin: Interrupt.
It's rude and disrespectful.

Rule: Concentrate on what is being said.
Do not plan your responses while listening – do not talk until the other person stops talking – control your ego – practice patience.

Sin: Criticize/ridicule/sarcastic
It is cruel and purposeless to act this way.

Rule: Address mistakes not personalities.
Focus on the good things that people do. If an individual's behavior needs to be corrected, it is best accomplished through a constructive exchange of thoughts. Look for reasons to praise.

Sin: Talking down or being arrogant.
Arrogance will alienate you from others.

Rule: Acknowledge your imperfections.
If you are a great person it will be noticed without your announcement.

Accelerate your transition from a manager to a leader by becoming an effective communicator.

Use your communication skills to provide people with the knowledge and truth they need to succeed.

Totally share what you know and believe.

The 99% rule about total sharing through effective communications:

99% of all people will willingly work hard and commit to the organization and its people if leadership shares 99% of all they know, and then listens to people with 99% of their effort.

How to measure your communications:

When the lowest ranked individual in your organization feels the same sense of ownership and responsibility as the highest ranked individual, you have effectively shared – you have effectively communicated.

Involvement/Delegation
(Ingredients in the recipe for leadership)

The goal:
    A workforce filled with feelings of high self-esteem as a result of accomplishments that benefit both the individual and the organization.

The means:
- Totally sharing knowledge and truth
- Encouraging involvement
- Providing the foundation that encourages feelings of empowerment

The accomplishments people make are their means to achieving feelings of high self-esteem. Once the process starts it becomes self-perpetuating for as long as their leaders continue to support it. Although self-perpetuating once started, it requires assistance to get started. Leaders initiate the process by sharing knowledge and truth and stimulating people's willingness to become involved.

One way to help get people involved in the daily management of the organization is through effective delegation. Through effective delegation – not direction – people can share in the management of the organization.

True delegation is not a common practice for many managers. In fact, few managers really know what it is. Too many managers hand out assignments and give directions under the guise of delegation. Assignments and directions are very different from delegation, and the results achieved are very different as well. For example, if you want to practice true delegation you may choose a goal such as improving safety. But to effectively delegate this goal to someone you would not give an individual the task of counting the number of safety incidents by type, time period, function and circumstance, and then have the person report the information back to you for remedial actions. This would be an assignment – this is not delegation. In this situation you have clearly retained the authority and responsibility for safety improvements and you are using someone on your team to help gather information for you. There is nothing wrong with doing this, but this is not delegation – this will not begin the self-perpetuating cycle of accomplishments and high self-esteem that results in feelings of fulfillment. It will become one of your accomplishments and your means to achieving feelings of high self-esteem for yourself.

If you want to resolve the safety issues in this area while also encouraging empowerment – you would delegate the entire function rather than handing out an assignment.

An additional benefit to the use of delegation vs. assignment would be that you would not only gain a safer work area and be providing someone with feelings of involvement, accomplishment and high self-esteem, but you would also be grooming an individual for promotion.

If you want to truly delegate and gain all the benefits that come from delegation, you would take the following steps:

- Thoroughly educate the selected individual with all you know about the safety performance of the chosen area, the possible causes for accidents, and some possible solutions. You would make it clear that if the person finds things to be different than your analysis, he or she has the authority to take the actions necessary to achieve improvements within the agreed upon limits of his or her authority.
- The agreed upon limits of authority usually consist of a budget, work hours, awareness of intended process, procedure or policy changes, and any disciplining that may be needed.
- You would agree on the goal.
- The person would have to be allowed sufficient time to review accidents, talk to people, conduct meetings and seek out alternatives.
- The person would need to be instructed to develop a tracking method to ensure the actions being taken are providing positive results.
- The person would have to provide you with periodic updates to ensure accountability and support.
- The person would have to understand that his or her performance will be measured by the results attained, not merely the effort expended.

Throughout this process the individual will be provided with knowledge and truth, supported, and held accountable as appropriate.

This is real delegation. This person will feel like he or she owns this responsibility and its results. This person will have a feeling of accomplishment and high self-esteem.

The manager who had the courage to act as a leader, to trust someone other than him or herself, and had the good sense to support the person along the road to success, will gain a great deal as well.

- The manager will have developed a "go to" person for future challenges.
- The problem will have been resolved while the department manager was doing something else, so his or her effectiveness will have been increased.
- Other members of the team will have witnessed what happened and the good results that followed, thus encouraging more people to seek challenges in the future.

To some managers the benefits do not out weigh the risks. These managers think that if the person fails then they the manager have failed – and they do not want to take that risk. These managers frequently do not have sufficient belief in anyone but themselves. These managers lack the courage to take risks.

What can I say except "a turtle does not make progress until it sticks its head out from under its shell" – it is very much the same for a manager.

Other managers resist delegating meaningful projects to people because they fear that if the person is successful, the person will get the credit and the manager might be considered unnecessary. In short, these managers are threatened by the success of their people, rather than feeling bolstered by the accomplishments of their team.

These are not managers destined to become leaders. These are not managers who will grow and achieve accomplishments that boost their self-esteem. If you want real success you must have the courage to trust in others – you must let go.

There are limits as to what can be delegated, however. A manager should not delegate:

- projects that might require disciplining an individual or group of individuals –disciplining should remain with the manager,
- small annoying jobs that the manager just does not like to do – this would be dumping, not delegating. This does not mean you can't assign jobs such as these to someone else – but don't call it delegating – call it what it is,
- functions which are beyond a team member's capability to carry out – such as developing a one-year manufacturing plan,
- functions which the manager just can't bring him or herself to let go – for example, ensuring on-time customer delivery might be something that the manager believes he or she should be doing personally.

Additionally, you need to remember that no matter how much you delegate functions to others, you continue to be ultimately responsible. You can share authority and responsibility – but you cannot give it away completely – nor should you want to.

Empowerment

(An ingredient in the recipe for leadership)

Clearly one of the major buzzwords of the last two decades has been empowerment. But what exactly is it?

Empowerment is a feeling.
It is a feeling that one has control over results.

Thus, if empowerment is a feeling rather than a tangible thing or fact – and if it is accepted to be the ultimate driving force to organizational improvement – then empowerment gives further proof to the belief that feelings are more important than facts.

Feelings drive actions – facts record them.

So how does one get these feelings?
Empowerment is the result of knowledge, truth, involvement, delegation, support, accountability and all the other ingredients of leadership. It is not a management program. It cannot be demanded.

It comes from within a person when that individual has a feeling of control over the events of his or her life – when a sense of ownership and responsibility is felt.

Empowerment encourages increased creativity, commitment and determination. Empowerment is a feeling that every manager in every company wishes was evident in each and every individual within the company.

Can you identify anyone in your organization that feels fully empowered? That is, a person who accepts full responsibility for the events of his or her work life – a person who takes needed actions without being told to do so?

Your list may possibly include the president of your company, a particular manager in your company, the janitor in your company, or maybe you. The title does not really matter. Anyone can feel empowered under the right circumstances. Feelings of empowerment are not specific to positions of power.

However, people who feel empowered often rise to positions of power.

The magic of empowerment is that these feelings are not based upon who you are or what you do – they are based upon how you feel about who you are and what you do.

These feelings about who you are and what you do can be greatly enhanced by an inspirational leader. A leader who provides opportunities for accomplishment, knowledge, truth, involvement, accountability, support and inspiration can encourage people to accept ownership for the challenges that lie before each individual.

True leaders know that feelings of empowerment are impossible without feelings of high self-esteem. True leaders know that feelings of high self-esteem are impossible without accomplishments.

Each of us has the ability to inspire and encourage feelings of empowerment – feelings that can make a difference in the lives of the people with whom we work.

Here are just some of the ways you can do this.

- Help people to accept challenges and achieve accomplishments. Help to remove the fear and provide support as needed.
- Help people to realize that they can never feel fulfilled until they learn to accept responsibility for the challenges that are ahead of them. No one can fulfill someone else by doing something for that person. Fulfillment can only be achieved from within when an individual accomplishes something of significance for him or herself.
- Help people to realize that their acceptance of responsibility makes it possible to overcome those things previously thought to be out of their control.
- Help people to understand that a person feels best about him or herself when he or she is doing things that are courageous, important and beneficial to themselves and the people around them.
- Help people to realize that blaming others for the unwanted events of their lives, and demanding that others do the things that will resolve their problems is to put one's destiny in control of someone else – it is the role of a victim – the role of hopelessness. It only makes things worse.
- Help people to accept the fact that one must take on challenges and responsibilities in order to grow.

- Help people to realize that by setting incremental goals aimed at resolving large problems, they are controlling some of the events of their lives.
- Help people to realize that the work they do is meaningful – that the accomplishments they make are needed – that they are contributing to a better organization and that the contributions will benefit themselves and the people within the organization.

"The human race is the story of men and women selling themselves short."

Abraham Maslow

What would you do?

Harry the supervisor is failing in his job. His boss wants more production and fewer problems. His team wants fewer demands and more money.

Harry feels caught in the middle.

No one on his team gets excited about anything that is associated with greater performance. People only care about their paychecks, their vacations, and how to avoid hard work.

The general attitude is to do as little as possible without getting into trouble. Whenever Harry tries to motivate people, the results are short-lived at best.

He has tried:

- Pep talks
- Monetary incentives
- Threats
- Punishment

Nothing has had lasting results. Morale is low and people just don't care. Harry thinks he has tried everything, so now he just goes about his business with little motivation to do anything while waiting for the axe to fall on him.

But has Harry really tried everything? No! He has not tried to change himself.

The answers that Harry is looking for lie within the lack of ownership and self-esteem people are feeling, and how Harry contributes to this situation.

Harry needs to focus on:

- Sharing all he knows as if it were the right of the people and his obligation to do so. That is, begin to treat the people like partners.
- Showing trust in people – delegating as much as possible – asking people for their opinions – allowing people to follow through on their ideas and then supporting them.
- Actively listening with empathy and energy.
- Helping people to realize their work is meaningful and each person is important.
- Holding each individual accountable to achieve what he or she is capable of doing and then recognizing the accomplishments each is making.

Effective work teams are the result of effective leaders who create effective opportunities to contribute and make meaningful accomplishments.

Harry must transition from a manager to a leader. He must become a leader who inspires rather than controls – who encourages feelings of ownership, empowerment and high self-esteem.

<u>Sharing Management</u>
(An ingredient in the recipe for leadership)

<u>A common scenario:</u>
Management establishes standards and methods for people to achieve and uses rewards or punishment in order to get people to work in accordance with these standards and methods.

<u>A better scenario:</u>
Management shares all they know about the needs of the organization and then encourages people's creativity. Management asks each individual to help establish his or her own standards and methods in support of the organization's needs. Management supports each individual to achieve the standards each individual has established and thereby helps the organization achieve its goals.

Which scenario do you think will have greater buy-in, follow-through and success?

<u>The Premise:</u>
*Management does not have complete
control over situations or people.
The best a manager can hope for is influence
that inspires people to contribute.
Influence is accomplished through
involvement, not demands.*

- Influence over a person is possible only if a person is willing to be influenced.

- A willingness to be influenced is a result of feeling that the direction is correct and the leader can be trusted.
- Feelings of correctness are enhanced by an opportunity to participate in the selection of the direction.
- An opportunity to participate in the selection of a direction is enhanced by management having the skills needed to effectively communicate the needs of the organization and the ability to guide people through the involvement process.

Real leaders know how to share the management of the organization with people.

- Real leaders share knowledge and truth.
- Real leaders encourage empowerment and effectively delegate functions.
- Real leaders ask people for their opinions and their help.
- Real leaders support people's efforts.
- Real leaders inspire people to accept challenges.
- Real leaders are open and honest.

Some managers believe that tight controls and directives are the only means of maintaining a focused team that works diligently on the goals of the company. These managers are intimidated by the thought of sharing the establishment and execution of plans with the people who carryout the plans.

Yet, somewhat like a jockey on a racing horse, when the reins are held tightly to ensure control, the horse is not able to run at full gallop – the race could be lost because of the controls.

Real leaders have the courage to become somewhat vulnerable. They share and accept opposing ideas. They seek to win the race by providing greater slack on the reins. They trust – as does the jockey on the horse – that if they share knowledge, truth and the opportunity for involvement, (*oats, water and exercise*) – the direction chosen will be straight and narrow.

It has been my experience that people in the workforce frequently come to the same conclusions, and make the same decisions as their manager when they are provided with the same information. If you are a manager who provides knowledge and truth, and you are true to your values, you will find much more support for the ideas that are in the best interests of the organization and its people than you might think. In other words, real leaders know that when they do their job correctly there are few risks in sharing the management of the company with the people who work within the company.

It is very smart for a leader to manage people in such a manner. As previously stated, management really does not have total control over people if the people choose not to line-up with the thought process. Encouraging people to get in line with the thought process through knowledge, truth and the opportunity to be involved promotes a great amount of unity and single-mindedness.

Water runs down a hill certain of achieving its destiny at the bottom by always taking the path of least resistance around rocks, trees and bushes. So too, must management keep its sight on the goals ahead while also seeking the paths of least resistance through ideas, methods, differences of opinion, personal ambitions, procedures, policies, processes and rules. It is only through open involvement, compromise and negotiations that management can be sure of reaching its goals. It is only in this way that the goals of the organization, the goals of managers and the goals of the workforce become identical and pursued by each person within the organization. Only in this way does an organization achieve unity and single-minded efforts for continuous improvement.

I have met many so-called dynamic managers who would read of this need to compromise methods and ideas with people and conclude that it is a sign of weakness.

However, if knowledge and truth are being shared with each individual as if each individual were a partner in the company, there is little risk of a workforce believing in one direction while management believes in another. If these dynamic managers were truly doing their jobs correctly, they would not have to fear this sharing process and be forced to resort to the manipulation of people as their means to having their way of thinking carried out.

Manipulation, spinning, or forcing one's will upon others without their complete buy-in is lazy and reckless management. Providing knowledge, truth, empowerment, involvement, support and effective accountability requires a great deal more energy, courage and skill – but it is far more effective. It is anything but a sign of weakness.

Rather it is a weakness:

- to be so insecure in one's management position that people's involvement is a threat,
- to take the easy way out of managing by forcing one's will upon others rather than teaching and encouraging people to share in the management of the organization.

True leaders are truly strong of character and will. True leadership requires:

- one to give of him or herself before demanding from others,
- one to seek to understand others before expecting to be understood,
- a belief in the value of people,
- excellent communication skills – especially listening,
- energy, determination, and focus,
- real confidence,
- real courage,
- real sharing.

Characteristics of a leader who shares management with people:

- <u>Trusting.</u> This manager believes people with whom he or she has shared knowledge and truth will openly and honestly give of themselves for the good of the organization.

- <u>Wise.</u> This manager knows the best decisions are a result of many varied points of view from many different people. This manager knows no single person could consider as many alternatives as a group of people.
- <u>Considerate.</u> This manager helps people cope with the difficulties and stress that can be created by the give and take process of compromising and agreeing upon a direction. This manager knows how to keep issues focused and objective, while being empathetic toward the people whose ideas are not chosen.
- <u>Intuitive.</u> This manager quickly recognizes ideas that should be pursued. This manager knows ideas that are win/win for all parties involved are ideas that will be successfully carried out.
- <u>Energetic.</u> This manager knows the involvement process requires more energy and determination than working alone. This manager maintains his or her physical, intellectual and emotional health.
- <u>Inspirational.</u> This manager realizes that one of the most important roles of a leader is to provide inspiration. This manager is an example of correctness, work ethics and is able to keep problems in perspective. This manager finds the good in each situation.
- <u>Focused.</u> This manager never loses sight of the goal – that goal being to make the organization more prosperous and provide opportunities for the

people to achieve feelings of high self-esteem and fulfillment.

- <u>Self-Disciplined.</u> This manager effectively guides the process without giving in to the temptation of taking it over. This manager facilitates the process and sacrifices for the good of the organization and its people. This manager keeps people on track, keeps people involved, and keeps people feeling good about themselves and the work they are doing.

- <u>Flexible.</u> This manager knows the skills used in participation planning are different than the skills needed to successfully execute the plan. This manager knows he or she must be authoritative once the plan and methods are agreed upon. This manager is able to provide whatever style is needed in a situational manner.

<u>Helping to Resolve Problems</u>
(An ingredient in the recipe for leadership)

You show true concern for people

You actively provide knowledge and truth

You become skilled at effective communications
– especially listening

You effectively delegate, empower and help to build
people's self-esteem

You encourage people to accept challenges and
achieve accomplishments

You involve people in the management
of the organization

You are true to your values and filled with integrity

Is that enough?
Are you through?

<u>No!</u>
Now you must provide support by teaching people
how to overcome the obstacles they will encounter
when working toward shared goals and individual
accomplishments.
When people feel stifled – they <u>are</u> stifled.
When people feel they lack the ability to affect
change – they <u>do</u> lack the ability.

Feelings are more important than facts!

All the hard work in the world cannot counter the effects of people feeling they cannot and do not make a difference. When they feel this way – it is this way.

When people feel this way – when they feel unable to help themselves – you need to help them to help themselves. You need to change how they feel about the situation. But you do not resolve problems for them – you resolve problems with them.

By solving problems with people rather than for people, individuals will learn how to resolve these obstacles for themselves in the future. Additionally, they will be better able to maintain their self-esteem since they are taking care of their own problems.

The recommended support you should be providing is a combination of:

a. graciousness,
b. empathy,
c. investigating & planning,
d. implementing & following up,
e. accountability.

Graciousness:
- You start by "rolling out the red carpet" for them. You are understanding and totally involved in the problem.
- You ensure you are always Available, Approachable and Attentive. (The 3A's)

- You eliminate the "red tape". As the manager, only you can do this.
- You ensure you are without bias. You are open to different beliefs and different points of view, but you never compromise your values or the wellbeing of the organization and its people.

Empathic:
- You join forces. The person's problem becomes your problem. You accept this because it will eventually effect the organization, its people, and the fulfillment of the individual if the problem is allowed to continue.

Investigating & planning:
- You begin to break down the problem into bite-size opportunities for accomplishment.
- You lead the process through a series of open-ended questions. That is, questions that cannot be answered by a simple yes or no. The person must explain and detail the problem.
- You ask the person what he or she thinks should be done.
- You guide the thinking if the answers are all the responsibility of someone else to carry out.
- You agree on what this person with the problem can accomplish and how it can be accomplished.
- You agree on what outside assistance the person will need.
- You agree on what assistance you will provide.
- You agree on the need for gathering facts.
- You agree on a plan and timetable to begin the corrective actions.

<u>Implementation & follow up:</u>
- You begin the required actions.
- You monitor results and hold all applicable individuals accountable to carryout the plan as agreed upon.
- You continue to give guidance and support as appropriate.

Once again there are many managers who do not see the need for this type of support. Their thought process goes something like this: "The people have their jobs and I have my job. They have their problems, and I have my problems. I don't ask them to solve my problems, so they should not expect that I should help them solve their problems. Let them learn how to take care of themselves. If they can't do the job or take care of themselves, I'll find people who can."

Sound familiar?

I hope not. This is not managing, and this is definitely not leading. These types of managers should not be in the position of management.

It's true a workforce that is self-sufficient is the ultimate goal – but it is not true that it can get that way without the guidance of a leader.

How can a leader personally address every problem when there are so many of them? The answer is that he or she cannot. If the leader is doing his or her job correctly, he or she should not have to.

There are 3 basic types of problems:

1. Relatively large, usually costly and always very frustrating problems that require the leader's involvement to resolve. For these types of problems the leader must find the time to facilitate the problem as described on the previous page.
2. Smaller, less costly and less frustrating problems that go on each day which the workforce is normally able to resolve without the help of the leader, (providing the leader has been sharing knowledge and truth, and encouraging involvement and empowerment).
3. Smaller, less costly, but very frustrating problems that go on each day which the workforce does not have the wherewithal to resolve. These types of problems need the help of the leader, yet they can easily get lost in the priority order of activities.

For example, I became aware of a situation in which a machine operator was missing a tool he needed intermittently throughout the course of each day. He told his boss on numerous occasions, but because the operator was able to borrow the tool each time from a co-worker the boss did not feel the pressure to quickly respond. In fact, it was a low priority given all the other problems with which he was dealing.

The machine operator, on the other hand, found this to be very aggravating and frustrating. In spite of all the many good things this supervisor did daily, he was now sending a very clear message to this individual that he was not important and that his work did not need to be performed at peak efficiency.

This message negatively effected many decisions that the machine operator made daily as he was now guided by the thought that neither he nor his efficiency was important. Obviously, this is not a good situation. What is not obvious, however, is that this scenario is played out hundreds of times daily in thousands of businesses.

What should be happening is quite the opposite. It should be clearly known by everyone that all problems are serious, all people are important and peak efficiency is absolutely necessary.

This opposite message could have been easily given in this example if the boss simply acted immediately. In an environment in which people's needs and problems are acted upon immediately, people will know that they and the job they do are important.

This must always be the belief.

You need to become "Facilitator Man" – not "Superman".

You need to solve problems, but you cannot get caught in the trap of solving problems for people while they simply point them out. This is a paternalistic management style that weakens people and eventually burns out the manager.

Only "Superman" could excel in this type of environment.

Your role as "Facilitator Man" is to solve problems <u>with</u> people.

You need to become:

- Organizer of problem-solving activities,
- Teacher, catalyst, and source of knowledge to others,
- Leader and visionary for a better way,
- Sounding board and voice of reason,
- Protector of the belief that people need support, and people need to feel important,
- Director, but only as necessary,
- The manager that neither does things for people – nor dumps the problem back onto people – but rather, the manager that resolves problems with people.

In the example of the missing tool, the supervisor should have immediately asked the person to accept the job of making a complete tool inventory. The person could have then been asked to write and present the purchase orders for any needed tools to the supervisor for his approval.

With these actions the immediate problem could have been immediately resolved while also taking the preventative action of developing a complete tool inventory to prevent missing tools in the future. Additionally, by teaching the person how to solve the problem he could have provided an opportunity for accomplishment and growth for the machine operator.

From these simple actions the person would have felt:

- he and the work he does are important,
- efficiency is important,

- trusted,
- a sense of accomplishment,
- a boost to his self-esteem.

Start now:
- Actively listen to people's requests for support regardless of the presentation.
- Share problems with people and guide them through the actions they need to take.
- Become "Facilitator Man" – not "Superman".
- Support people by showing them how they can help themselves.
- Practice the 3 A's.
- Remove the "red tape" if it is getting in the way.
- Act immediately, even if it is just to write down the problem for follow-up at a later date.
- Break down the problems into incremental opportunities for accomplishment and put some preventative actions in place as well.
- Thank the individual for making you aware of the problem.

Progress Through Decisions
(An ingredient in the recipe for leadership)

Your current work environment is a result of past decisions.
Your future work environment will be the result of decisions being made today.

Things don't just happen.
There are reasons for everything.

Real leaders know that they can influence the future through the decisions they make today.

Every leader's goal should be to make as many well thought-out decisions as can possibly be made. If you want the best results from the decisions you make, you need to practice the best procedures of decision-making.

- As much as possible, you should be making decisions in a collaborative atmosphere where people are aware of the goals and encouraged to contribute their thoughts.
- You should be encouraging differences of opinion, actively listening and taking decisive actions.
- You should be collecting data and making fact-based decisions.

One of the major goals requiring decisive actions for any leader is to increase profits for his or her organization. To that end leaders are continuously looking for ways to improve worker efficiency as one of the many initiatives in a long list of goals. Too often, however, I've seen managers jump to quick conclusions, rather than making well thought-out and collaborative decisions as to how to improve efficiency. Too often I have witnessed knee-jerk reactions assuming that there is a need to "kick some butt", for example, or single out the worst performing people, and/or give rewards to those who are performing well.

Too many managers call this being decisive, proactive and dynamic. Too many managers believe they are brilliant for coming to these conclusions so quickly and easily.

I call it lazy, impulsive and reckless. I think these managers are anything but brilliant. I give them credit for knowing that actions are needed, but then they fail to make well-thought-out, collaborative decisions.

They look at complex issues and instantly come up with simple solutions. But they are nearly always wrong.

The average, "less brilliant" manager needs to follow the proper steps of good decision making. These "less gifted managers" realize that for every complex problem there is usually a complex solution. These managers seek to fully understand the many factors that are at the root of problems.

For example, a true leader seeking to improve efficiencies would:

- review the 3E's – that is:
  a. Are the people and supervisors properly Educated?
  b. Is the Equipment adequate?
  c. Are the processes being Executed exactly as intended?
- if the answer to any of the above questions is no, true leaders seek the help of others to remedy the situation,
- if equipment is found to be inadequate, for example, true leaders would ask why it is as it is at least 5 times,
  a. Why is the equipment inadequate? – possible answer: because it was not maintained,
  b. Why was it not maintained? – because schedule requirements did not allow enough time for preventative maintenance,
  c. Why did schedule requirements not allow enough time? – because capacity planning was not adequately performed,
  d. Why was capacity planning not adequately performed? – because the planning department did not think it was necessary,
  e. Why did the planning department think that it was not necessary? – because nobody ever complained about too much or too little work,

As you might imagine, this could go on for a while until the root cause is identified. The so-called brilliant manager may have also discovered the problem of ineffective equipment, and then immediately punished the people responsible for not maintaining the equipment – a typical "knee-jerk" reaction. But punishment will not solve the problem because the people responsible are unable to carry out their jobs due to the current situation.

Nevertheless, the brilliant manager will go away thinking he or she did a great job resolving this problem, when in fact nothing was resolved at all. Either customer commitments or the machinery upkeep will continue to suffer depending on the decision that is made at any given point in time.

The "less brilliant" manager who takes the time to uncover the root cause of this problem will help the production supervisor and his team by educating the planning department. In the future capacity planning will be carried out and maintenance personnel will be able to adequately do their jobs. This is effective decision-making. This is achieving lasting improvements. This is improving the company. This is progress through decisions.

Holding People Accountable
(An ingredient in the recipe for leadership)

Encouraging people's creativity while also
maintaining disciplined behavior.
Can these activities co-exist?

Helping people achieve a high self-esteem while also
holding them accountable.
Can these two activities co-exist?

Yes!
These things can and must co-exist.

An effective manager/worker relationship
is a close and trusting relationship that is based
upon clearly defined values and standards that are
understood and supported by each.

- People must know that you care about them and
  their needs – but that you expect them to accept
  responsibility for their actions and results.
- People must know of your values and standards,
  and believe that they are good and right for the
  organization and each individual within the
  organization – but they must also know these values
  and standards can never be compromised.
- People must know that you seek to help each person
  achieve success – and that you believe it is best
  accomplished by also ensuring the organization's
  success.

- People must know that you seek to achieve the organization's success – and that you do this by helping each individual within the organization achieve his or her success.
- People must know that you protect each individual's right to open and free expression – but if it becomes harmful to the organization and its people, you will not allow it to continue.
- People must know that you will always compromise on the creation of plans and methods – but never on the execution of an agreed upon plan or method.
- People must know you are open, honest, trusting and trustworthy – and that you expect the same from each individual in return.
- People must know you are resolute in your mission – and expect the same from them.
- People must know that you will always support each individual's need for accomplishment – and will also hold them accountable to work to their potential.
- People must know that you will never be permissive of behavior that is not in the best interest of the organization – and that you will help people to avoid misbehavior.

But how can an entire team or entire workforce know so much about your values and standards?

- *You must state them frequently,*
- *explain them always,*
- *live them exactly.*

"Who you are speaks so loudly that I cannot hear what you say."
Ralph Waldo Emerson

Your authority needs to be based on your values and leadership skills – as well as your reputation for always doing what is right for the organization and its people.

Let the support of these things speak for you through your words and actions.

When it comes to exercising your authority over people you should be a disciplinarian not a dictator.

Never give in to the quick-fix methods of fear or paternalistic rewards as a dictator would. These activities will not achieve a disciplined and motivated team. They create a dependent team.

Techniques such as these indicate a lack of competence. They reflect laziness. They are a sure-fail method for achieving unity and single-minded efforts toward goals.

When a manager attempts to hold people accountable by controlling activities and then punishing or rewarding results, he or she is managing people as if they were machines. This type of manager greases and oils the people, (punishes or rewards them), but he or she does not spend sufficient time establishing trusting relationships based on values and standards.

These managers convince themselves that this is proper because they can state examples of when they tried to share knowledge and truth only to be let down by the results. They never consider that people don't trust them and consequently do not give of themselves because the leadership behavior is not carried out consistently.

These managers continue their efforts to control people through manipulative or punitive tactics. They believe it is all that will work for them and ironically, because they have not been managing correctly, these tactics really are the only ways they can expect to get anything accomplished.

People who are managed in situations such as this rarely get the opportunity to achieve greatness because they are not inspired to work to their potential. *They do what is accepted rather than what is possible.* They are controlled to perform to a level determined to be adequate by the manager.

On the other end of accountability failure are the supervisors who have gotten so friendly with their team members that maintaining a no nonsense focus on priorities has become very difficult.

In this situation the people do not view their supervisor as the keeper of justice with values and high standards, but rather a friend who accepts their behavior unconditionally. This supervisor is reluctant to take remedial actions for fear of losing the people's friendship. This is a manager who thinks closeness and harmony cannot co-exist with efforts to improve efficiency, quality and productivity. This is a manager who does not realize that people need to satisfy their need for accomplishment and high self-esteem – not gain their boss as a friend. In fact, a manager that acts like this is really no friend at all.

Managers who are also leaders drive for continuous improvements, commitment and sacrifices from people. Managers who are also leaders know people need challenges, knowledge, truth, involvement, empowerment, support and accountability.

True leaders are understanding and empathetic –
but they are never permissive. True leaders
understand the nature of their authority.

Authority

What is this thing we call authority? Is it a gift, is it demanded, or is it earned?

If you are in management you have been given some amount authority over others. But what happens next is dependent on your effectiveness and the people you manage. Some managers give away their authority rather than building upon it. These are managers who do not act against people who are behaving improperly, or who do not take needed improvement actions relative to the job.

Other managers give their authority away by being unfair, inconsistent or managing people in a manner that does not provide for their need for accomplishment and high self-esteem. People will resist the authority of someone who apparently has little concern for them.

The given authority of a manager can and should be cultivated. This is possible when people allow it to be so. That is, when a manager transforms to a leader, his or her authority is greatly increased because people have chosen to follow. Thus, although authority appears to be given – true authority is earned – cannot be demanded – and is given to those who lead by those who choose to follow.

A manager who understands what it means to be a leader is a manager who understands that an *effective manager/worker relationship is a close and trusting relationship that is based upon clearly defined values and standards that are understood and supported by each.*

An example of a close and trusting relationship that is guided by values and standards might be:

You have a team member named Jim with several years of good service who is performing poorly of late. You meet with Jim to discuss the situation. In the meeting you clearly state your disappointment with his performance and ask why it has been slipping. Jim begins to share that he and his wife are planning to separate and he is unable to accept the situation. Additionally, he admits that he is under financial pressure and has begun to drink alcohol to excess as a way of escaping his problems. During the conversation he begins to cry and tell you that he needs your help so that he doesn't lose his job on top of all his other problems.

What would you do?

- *"Don't worry about a thing. I'll cover for you until you can get things straightened out."*
  Would this be the proper response?
  <u>No.</u> This is permissiveness, and permissiveness is <u>never</u> the correct choice. You would be lowering your standards and compromising your values. Additionally, this does not really help Jim to get his problem resolved. He will have little motivation to change his behavior, as you would be enabling him to continue without consequence.

- *"Why don't you try to get yourself together – it's not the end of the world. These things happen to everyone. So pick up the pieces and get back on track."*
  Would this be an acceptable response?
  <u>No.</u> To Jim it is the end of the world. It will not help to make light of it. You would be showing little empathy or concern – you would not be doing anything to correct his poor performance.

- *"I know you've got serious problems, but I cannot cut you any slack. We have a business to run, so if you do not shape up immediately, I'll have to let you go."*
  Would this be the right response?
  <u>No.</u> Although you would be acknowledging the seriousness of the situation and are insisting on improved performance, it could result in his discharge if he resists the tough guy tactics. He may also be unable to resolve the situation without

help. You could lose a normally good worker for a temporary situation. Even if he did make a turnaround he would lose trust in you and would be difficult to manager in the future.

- *"Jim, I'm very concerned about your situation and job performance. I wish I could make it better for you – but I can't – only you can make it better, and I insist you do so. However, I would like to help by having the company pay for some professional counseling. I will not accept excessive drinking as a viable reason for your poor performance so I insist you take advantage of this offer and immediately turn around your performance. We will talk again next week. Now let's get started."*

Is this the proper response?

<u>Of course it is.</u> It will do no good to give in to his tendency to slack off and bury himself in self-pity and alcohol. By insisting that he maintain his focus on the job he may be able to get his mind off some of his problems. By paying for the professional counseling you are showing trust and concern for him as well as displaying your opinion of his importance to the organization.

A true leader cannot condone inappropriate behavior or poor performance – but he or she does not leave people out in the cold either. A true leader does this for:

- the individual,
- the organization,
- the people within the organization,
- his or her own values.

A true leader does not consider him or herself to be a hero or heroine. He or she simply cares about people and the organization.

When people have problems:
- Treat them as you would a member of your immediate family,
- Ensure you are Available, Approachable, Attentive (the 3A's),
- Help people to express themselves,
- Be empathetic,
- Leave your biases behind,
- Ask questions until you are sure you understand the situation,
- Maintain your values and high standards.

Consequences
(An ingredient in the recipe for leadership)

Will everybody immediately respond to your leadership, work to his or her potential, and seek fulfillment through accomplishments? Certainly not. In any organization there will be some people who take longer to respond to this leadership style and a few who never do.

So while you continue to manage as a true leader, for these few people you will need to also apply some additional and immediate consequences.

All people do things for their own reasons.
Consequently you need to know what has the most effect on each individual.

- Avoidance of punishment
- Opportunity for a reward
- Recognition from peers and superiors

Nearly anyone will respond to one or more of the above motivators no matter what their expectations. Yet the full-time application of these three motivators is not the ultimate goal of a manager transitioning to leader. These motivators are aimed at the lower level needs of people. Although they are sometimes necessary when people in the workforce are transitioning from employees into partners, the higher level needs of self-esteem and self-actualization are still the ultimate goal.

Additionally, if after a reasonable amount of time the use of the lower level motivators in conjunction with the ingredients to leadership do not result in feelings of partnership, the manager should make a close examination of him or herself, as well as the individual involved. This would be an indication that he or she is not effectively transitioning from manager to leader, and/or the individual is part of a small group of people who never transition into a partner relationship. In either case, remedial actions are needed.

When deciding to use lower level motivators you need to ensure your thinking and beliefs are proper. That is, you should:

- Believe that people deserve more attention than just the issuance of a paycheck. With the use of these three motivators people will receive some acknowledgement for the things they do until they begin to rise above these basic needs to the higher level needs of self-esteem and self-actualization.
- Believe that people are naturally motivated for their own reasons – not necessarily management's reasons.
- Believe that these motivators, if carried out sincerely, can help people begin to make the connection that what is good for the organization is also good for the people within the organization – and vice versa.
- Believe that even when people are receiving satisfaction from their higher level needs as a

result of accomplishments, some people also need occasional rewards to help keep them on track – especially if they are new to this leadership style.

- Believe that people are basically good – but this is not enough. People need leadership and direction, and the initial use of these motivators can help that process get started.

The reason tangible consequences such as these are effective is quite simple:

- Good consequences following good behavior encourage a person to repeat that behavior.
- Bad consequences following bad behavior discourage a person from repeating that behavior.

But whether it is good behavior you are rewarding, or bad behavior you are discouraging, the key to your success in using these methods, as well as making it possible to eventually transition to higher level motivators, is the <u>sincerity</u> with which you carry them out.

The person must trust you and your values. The person must see that you provide consequences for his or her behavior because you always want what is best for the organization and its people. The person must understand that the encouragement of his or her proper behavior with tangible consequences helps to accomplish this end goal.

Applying consequences for actions should always be accompanied with expressions of sincere gratitude for good behavior, or sincere disappointment for improper behavior.

Expressions of sincere gratitude are:
- Friendly
- Concerned
- Immediate
- Educational
- Specific

Expressions of sincere disappointment are:
- Friendly
- Concerned
- Immediate
- Empathetic
- Resolute

Sincere words of gratitude or
disappointment can be very powerful tools.

Feelings of appreciation are always needed – and
they always encourage more good performance.

Consequences for behavior are necessary in order
to avoid people thinking you don't care or have not
noticed.

If they believe either of the two, they will also not
care.

When it comes to consequences for behavior:

"Nothing is so unfair as the equal treatment of unequals."
The One Minute Manager by Ken Blanchard

<u>Holding Yourself Accountable</u>
(An ingredient in the recipe for leadership)

A real leader knows that accountability starts with him or herself. As a leader you are responsible to ensure your physical, intellectual and emotional fitness to perform your duties. To neglect any of these vital areas is to ensure limited capabilities. Without your physical fitness, for example, you will not have the energy to grow from a manager to a leader.

Once again, *people do things for their own reasons*. So if you need a reason to take your own health seriously, just look around at those people who do not.

As a minimum, try the following simple activities aimed at improving your physical health:

- Regular sleep pattern – preferably early to bed and early to rise – and at least 7-8 hours each night,
- Consistent exercise program – at least 30 minutes of some vigorous activity performed no less than 3-4 times per week,
- Proper eating habits - not over-eating, not under-eating – high fiber and low fat diet – a minimal amount of junk food,
- Moderate use of alcohol – no smoking – no drugs of any kind,
- Maintain a healthy weight and get yearly physical examinations,
- Laugh at least once per day and work hard at maintaining an active social life with meaningful relationships,

- Learn to relax and have fun.

If you choose to follow something less than the simple recommendations above, there will be some degree of adverse effect.

Don't settle for anything less than what you can be.

Intellectual fitness is your responsibility as well. You are responsible to the organization and its people to self-educate. It is not the organization's responsibility to provide you with continuous opportunities and to increase your education, although many organizations do offer various types of intellectual opportunities.

Another simple list of recommendations relative to ensuring intellectual fitness would be:

- Technical or managerial seminars, workshops, and/or subscriptions to magazines or newsletters. – Many organizations will pay for these activities, but whether or not your organization does cover these expenses, it remains your responsibility to do some of these things.
- College level courses. – Many organizations also have tuition reimbursement programs and it makes little sense not to take advantage of such opportunities.
- In-plant training courses.
- Attention to everyday experiences and volunteering for new assignments.

Don't sell yourself short.

When it comes to emotional fitness, however, it is not as simple as making out a list to follow. If you are not emotionally stable, there may be little I can offer that will help. If you are stable, but sometimes troubled, then some of the following thoughts might be helpful.

Some examples that may indicate a need for you to improve your emotional health may be:

- people telling you that you are difficult to work with – and you know it's true,
- conflicts with other people a little too often,
- in a bad mood a little too frequently,
- feelings of being overwhelmed,
- feelings of inadequacy,
- losing your temper a little too frequently,
- dreading going to work, especially on Mondays,
- frequently feeling pressed for time,
- a strong need to escape.

This may not be an all-inclusive list, but hopefully it is helpful in identifying a need for change.

Emotional health can be the most crucial, yet most neglected of all the fitness factors. A person who has feelings such as listed above frequently keeps these feelings to him or herself and suffers in silence. This can be destructive for the person and the people with whom he or she works. It is a serious detriment to becoming a leader. If not addressed it can get worse as the feelings begin to self-perpetuate.

Some examples of the consequences of these feelings may be:

- difficulty focusing,
- self-absorption and lack of concern for others,
- unexplained and unproductive tangents,
- an inability to carry out assignments properly.

I am not a psychiatrist or qualified counselor, but let me offer you some observations that I have made throughout my career that could help.

- <u>Maintain perspective.</u>

Suppose you are a manager unable to meet production requirements and you begin to have feelings of inadequacy. What might be some things you could do to help?

Breaking down the problem into incremental opportunities for improvement may be one helpful action. That is, instead of viewing the many causes as problems – look at them as targets for improvement. Each time you accomplish one of the targets you are getting closer to resolving the entire situation and increasing your self-esteem.

a. break down the problem into incremental goals to be achieved,
b. take on each goal with energy, determination and excitement,
c. remind yourself that each time you achieve an incremental goal you are making your work-life better, the organization better and its people better,
d. get other people involved – share problems and successes with the people with whom you work

– after all, isn't that what partners are supposed to do?

e. trust in the abilities of the people with whom you work and believe in yourself,

f. work hard but try to have fun as you work – allow feelings of accomplishment to boost your self-esteem.

Don't waste valuable time on negative thoughts of hopelessness or inadequacy. These thoughts do nothing to help – these thoughts do nothing to empower you to act. Stay focused on the opportunities and believe in yourself.

It makes no sense not to.

*   <u>Do not act when you are feeling out of control – restrain yourself until you have calmed down.</u>
    A true leader does not make reactionary decisions while in a state of emotional stress. Leaders know that situations, facts and feelings are in a constant state of flux, so it makes sense to let the dust settle and make a decision that is true to your values and is best for the organization and its people.

    Actions taken during an emotional state could cause adverse side effects that can last long after the situation is subsided. Leaders do not cause increased damage by acting inappropriately.

*   <u>Laugh at least once per day.</u>
    A wonderfully successful and pleasurable way of controlling negative feelings is to laugh. Laughter

really can be the best medicine and making light of serious situations often times helps to clarify thoughts and needed actions. For example, look at the work of the late Bob Hope. His ability to make the troops laugh when faced with high levels of danger and stress performed minor miracles for the men and women in the audience.

(I know. I was one of those GI's he made laugh when there was sadness all around me. It helped a great deal.)

There is no reason why work should not also be fun. People need joy in their lives and work is as good a place as any to get it. Management goals such as efficiency and productivity are not in conflict with enjoyment. These things can and should co-exist.

Do not let a day pass you by in which you have not had some form of happiness and satisfaction. Each day of your life is gone forever once it has been lived. Live for the minute you are in – and the one that is coming up.

- Share your feelings.

  Although we are all different – we are also the same in many ways. We can learn a great deal from each other if we take the time to share our feelings. When you share your feelings with others you will frequently learn that the feelings you may be having are feelings that others have as well. The person with whom you share your feelings may have some advice that is helpful.

  Voice your fears and concerns. Release your

tensions and insecurities. Know that no one has to be alone if he or she chooses not to be. Know that if you share your feelings with others, others will share in return. Know that it is the sharing of weaknesses – not strengths – that endears people to one another.

- Exercise.
  We all know that exercise is important for maintaining our physical health. But it may be just as important for maintaining our emotional health as well. Regular exercise can reduce tensions as well as release natural chemicals that counter feelings of depression. Regular exercise can also be an accomplishment that provides feelings of high self-esteem.

- Understand the nature of stress and thereby effectively manage it.
  Stress does not exist outside of an individual. It is the interpretation of situations that cause feelings defined as stress within a person. The same situation experienced by two different people can have two different interpretations, two different levels of stress.
  To help control feelings of stress it is important to realize that stress is a result of interpretation. Interpretation is a result of our beliefs. Our beliefs are a result of our upbringing and experiences - but they can be changed or at least modified. So in addition to the recommendations already provided in this chapter, let me suggest that if you want to

control stress – try to control what you believe. Choose your thoughts and beliefs.

a. If you are feeling stressed – choose not to allow it - determine the interpretation that is causing it and change the belief that is behind it.

b. Do not resist the inevitability of change in your life – change is the only thing of which you can be sure.

c. Choose not to allow yourself the feeling of being a helpless victim. Accept responsibility and begin to change what you do not like.

d. Don't be afraid of the unknown. Everything in your life at this moment was once unknown by you at some time prior to this moment.

e. Choose to view new assignments as new opportunities to learn and accomplish.

f. Ensure you are as prepared as possible for all contingencies, but do not expect perfection.

g. Work hard at being competent in all you do. But don't feel inadequate if you are less competent than someone else. Keep working at it and appreciate the progress you are making.

h. Develop a wide variety of interests. Enjoy life to the fullest.

i. Work hard to achieve a high self-esteem by seeking opportunities for accomplishment. Transition from manager to leader and enjoy the process.

j. Determine what you do well and do it to the best of your abilities. Frequently, that which you do well is also that which you enjoy doing.

__Managing Your Manager__
(An ingredient in the recipe for leadership)

The transition to leader may require
that you effectively manage your boss.
You should be showing your supervisor the same
concern, knowledge, truth and support
that you show to the members of your team.

Since the boss is unique as each individual is, you need to get to know him or her as you would a member of your team. Since the boss is not more special – as each individual is not – you should not be giving him or her preferential treatment. A manager transitioning to a leader should be treating each individual with whom he or she comes in contact with respect, dignity, knowledge, truth and support – and no one should be given more respect, dignity, knowledge, truth and support than another.

You need to establish a trusting and open relationship with the boss just as you should be doing with team members. You need to get to know him or her as an individual. You need to listen carefully to how he or she feels and thinks about things. You need to treat the boss as a partner in your quest for excellence.

As with your team members you may feel a little vulnerable being totally open and honest with the boss. Nevertheless, you need to share your values, standards and goals with the boss as best you can.

You also need to accept any differences that you may have with the boss as beneficial, since varied views frequently improve end results – but, just as with members of your team, you should never compromise your values and standards.

- Differences are normal.
- Differences can be healthy.
- The right of each individual to think differently should be protected.
- Differences should be openly discussed and worked out until unity is achieved.

An example of a difference that could arise between you and your boss might be the methodology for improving performance of a work area. The beliefs each of you have about people, as well as the beliefs about the responsibilities of management, will determine your assumptions and methods for making the improvements.

Because you are a caring manager and leader, you firstly look to see if the higher level needs of the people are being satisfied. That is, is management providing knowledge, truth, involvement, empowerment, support and accountability? Do people have an opportunity to achieve and increase their level of self-esteem?

You would also look for the root causes of the identified problems. You would be looking at the situation with the 3E's (Education of the people, Equipment adequacy, Execution of the processes) in mind.

As an effective leader you do not believe poor performance is automatically a result of the team not caring about the job and therefore not working very hard to improve things.

However, your boss may disagree. He or she may believe that the team-members of the area are simply not working hard enough and just do not care enough. The boss may think that tighter controls and possibly the elimination of some "bad apples" are the actions that should be taken. He or she may have had experiences in the past that caused this belief – and as certain as you are in your beliefs – he or she could be just as certain.

What would you do?

- <u>Go out with a bang?</u> Stick to your opinions and carry out changes according to your beliefs regardless of what your boss believes?

  Although this is courageous and true to your values and beliefs, it could also be professional suicide. You can expect serious confrontations with the boss for being so defiant. Your values and caring ways should apply to everyone, including the boss. So to completely disregard his or her thoughts would be as wrong as if you treated a team member in this manner. Remember everyone is unique, but no one is special – not even you. You do not have the right to act in this manner. It would not be good for the organization and its people.

- <u>Give in to the boss in all areas where you differ?</u>
  Bite your tongue and not be true to your values and standards?
  Obviously, this cannot be the right thing to do either. Acting in this manner is not the way of a courageous leader or follower. You should be respectful of the boss's views but you do not have to assume them. To do this would also not be in the best interest of the organization and its people.

- <u>Skillfully balance the beliefs of the boss with the needs of the organization, its people, and your own values and standards?</u>
  Clearly, this is the only solution to the differences. This approach will accomplish the tasks and yet not violate the values and beliefs of either you or the boss. But it is easier said than done.

You will need to actively and empathetically listen to the boss and determine if any or all of what he or she believes is true. You owe that to him or her as you would owe that to a team member. At the same time you should be carrying out your own beliefs relative to the ingredients of leadership. You should report the findings from both scenarios. As portions of both beliefs are proven or disproved, you act accordingly and provide a fair and balanced report. You are open, honest, true to your values and yet supportive to the boss as you are to the members of your team.

In the above example we see that the boss was treated no more special than anyone else – yet, his or her uniqueness was acknowledged and treated with respect and fairness.

This is how you manage your manager.

You should be doing a few more things relative to establishing an effective relationship with the boss.

- Pay attention to what your boss is attempting to accomplish and help him or her to accomplish it. Just like you and everyone else in the organization, he or she needs the help of others to be successful. No one can achieve success without help.
- Praise your boss when it is deserved just as you would a team member. He or she also needs recognition and appreciation. They too need to build feelings of high self-esteem.
- Be informative without being a nuisance. Just like everyone else in the organization, he or she needs knowledge and truth. Totally sharing everything you know and believe applies to the boss as well.
- Never say no. If you believe an assignment to be impossible or wrong, state the complexities and your concerns, as well as your need for support – but then go out and give it your best. He or she may be asking for the impossible because that is what is needed. And as close as you come to achieving the impossible, the better off the organization and its people may be.
- Accept constructive criticism from the boss that is aimed at improving your performance. Be gracious and thankful for his or her concern. But if the criticism is not constructive, but rather abusive or cruel, state your disappointment in his or her behavior and chalk it up to his or her lack of

leadership skills. Not every boss you work for will be a great leader.

- Be eager to take on more work and more responsibility. This is something you not only do for the boss, but you do it for yourself, the organization and its people as well.
- Accept full responsibility for your actions, your words and results. As a leader with values beyond reproach, you can do nothing else.
- Be enthusiastic about everything you do. If you are going to do something, it makes no sense not to do it well and enthusiastically.
- Never say, "I told you so".
- Be assertive – not aggressive. Your values, standards, opinions, beliefs and everything that goes along with them are out in the open for everyone to see. You stand your ground, but you are not obnoxious or aggressive about it.
- Be as understanding with the boss as you would be with a team member. He or she can make mistakes just like anyone else – and just like anyone else, he or she may need a little tender loving care when feeling low.
- Work hard, ensure your own effectiveness, and self manage.

Perceptions
(An ingredient in the recipe for leadership)

Achieving leadership status requires a manager to carry out all the ingredients in the recipe. Clearly, these ingredients demand a great deal of focus and hard work. Yet, as hard as you may be working to provide truth, knowledge, empowerment, involvement, support and accountability – the perception of your efforts could be different. And perception equals reality in the mind of the perceiver.

Great leaders exist in the minds and hearts of the people who choose to follow – not in the person who deems him or herself to be a great leader.

It is more important how people perceive your leadership skills than it is how you perceive yourself.

You need to know how others view you.

- <u>Learn to be perceptive of others.</u>
  Are results as expected? Are people following your lead?
  If the answer to these questions is no, there is a good chance you are not perceived as intended. You need to find out why. You need to correct whatever is wrong.
  a. Try to get close to people – try to determine what they think about you.
  b. Listen actively and empathetically to people. Do not be selective in what you are willing to hear. Do not dismiss things you do not want to believe.

c. Be gracious with any criticism you may receive. If not, you will never hear any truthful feedback again.

d. Make adjustments and then listen again and again.

- Establish comfortable relationships.
  People need to feel comfortable with you before they will be completely honest with you about you.

- Continue to show people in all you do and say that your only motivation is to do what is best for the organization and its people.
  Show the people that any obstacle determined to be detrimental to the organization and its people will be assertively dealt with – even if it is you.

- Seek people's interpretation of your words and actions by asking open-ended questions.
  Let them know you need their opinions. Ask people what they think you said or what they think you did. Do not ask questions that merely require a yes or no answer such as "Do you understand what I said?" It is too easy to just say yes.

- Guard against thinking it is the responsibility of the people to perceive you properly.
  Like everyone else, you are unique – and like everyone else, you are not special. The burden of effective communications belongs to the communicator – not the person to whom the communication is aimed. Help people to understand your uniqueness by bridging the perception gap.

<u>Courage – Determination – Actions</u>
(Ingredients in the recipe for leadership)

The belief that leadership is achieved through the list of ingredients we have just discussed must be lived.

The belief that real success for a manager is a result of becoming a leader who is true to his or her values and standards must be lived.

The transition to leadership will not come to fruition if you simply put down this book and say to yourself that these are nice thoughts. I should pass them on to my associates.

Change starts from within and requires
courage, determination and *actions.*

If you believe that managing people and organizations is best accomplished through the total sharing of knowledge and truth, providing opportunities for involvement, empowering, delegating, supporting and accountability – you need to act with courage and determination to make it so.

If you believe that people need accomplishments and feelings of high self-esteem in their work life – then you must act with courage and determination to make it become a reality for the people with whom you work.

Remember:
- Feelings are more important than facts.
- An organization can be no greater than its people and its people can be no greater than their self-esteem.
- The realities of today were created in yesterday's decisions – the future is being created today.
- People's true beliefs determine their actions.
- People's actions will determine their success.
- Truth is the foundation of trust.
- Trust is the foundation of leadership.
- Accomplishments are the key to high self-esteem and fulfillment.
- You can make a difference.

"Nothing splendid has ever been achieved except by those who dared believe that something inside of them was superior to circumstances."
Bruce Barton

"If we all did the things we are capable of doing, we would literally astound ourselves."
Thomas Edison

"Life is the story of mankind selling themselves short."
Abraham Maslow

"The only security a person has is his ability to do a job uncommonly well."
Abraham Lincoln

The beliefs you have in yourself and others will determine your actions – choose your beliefs wisely.
Ed Gagnon

About the Author

Ed has been managing and applying the ingredients of leadership for more than 30 years. His practical experiences range from submarine construction to textiles, from first line supervisor the general manager of multiple plants, from responsibility for 80 people to leadership of over 1100 people, from sectional responsibility to full profit and loss responsibility for companies with more than $100,000,000 in annual sales.

When Ed speaks of what it takes to be an effective manager and leader he speaks from both training and experience. Throughout his career Ed has applied the ingredients discussed in the Recipe for Leadership with consistent success.

Whether it resulted in turning around failing cost centers or in achieving further improvements in successful organizations, Ed's application of the Recipe for Leadership has fostered the achievement of lasting and impressive accomplishments for both the people and the organization for which they worked.